A
SPINSTER'S TOUR THROUGH
NORTH WALES

in search of

THE
PICTURESQUE & SENTIMENTAL

Dedicated

without permission

TO HER
THREE BELOVED SISTERS
E. H. & A.

GOMER

First Impression - 1988

© Lt. Col. and Mrs. J. E. Little

ISBN 0 86383 412 4

Printed at the Gomer Press, Llandysul, Dyfed Wales

PREFACE

I never could *read* a preface so
I certainly w'ont *write* one.

'that's poz'.

Foxgloves:
Augusta Pearson Watercolour

BIOGRAPHICAL NOTE

The author was the second daughter of Caroline Lyons (sister of Admiral Lord Lyons—sometime H.M. Ambassador in Athens) and Henry Shepherd Pearson whose occupation is unknown but who had connections with the India Office.

She was born on 16 February 1829 and was baptised at Great Marlow on 24 March 1829. She was married on 13 October 1859 at Mitcham Parish Church to George Arthur Knightley Hownan and their only child—a son named Ernest Knightley—was born on 23 October 1860.

In 1873 her husband assumed the name of Little and inherited property at Newbold Pacey in Warwickshire. Augusta lived there until her death in 1922 at the age of 93, outliving her son who died in 1921.

Her great-grandson and his family at present occupy the house— and it was they who discovered this journal on the bookshelves— where it must have stood for the last 100 years.

*   *   *

A Glossary at the end of this book attempts to explain words and terminology in common usage in the middle of the nineteenth century and gives background information to places and buildings featured in the tour.

Acknowledgements

H.M.S.O.:   Lithographs of *The Euston Square Station*
                       and *The Britannia Bridge*

Area Record Office,
Gwynedd County Council,
Caernarfon: Lithographs of *The Departure*
                                Penrhyn Castle
                                Carnarvon Castle
                                The City of Bangor

National Library of Wales:
Watercolours by Rev. John Parker   *Picnic in the Rain*
                                Llyn Gwynant, near Beddgelert
                                Llanberis Pass

FOREWORD by Lady Anglesey

A Spinster's tour through North Wales in Search of the Picturesque and the Sentimental is Miss Augusta Pearson's account of a first visit there in 1853 aged 17. I first came to North Wales as a newly married woman nearly a hundred years later. Many of the places she visited and indeed many of the people she met are as recognisable today as they were 150 years ago.

She sent home to her three sisters left behind in London this shrewd, witty and delightfully illustrated record. The Sights that Must Not be Missed still include the Edwardian Castles and the summit of Snowdon. In 1853 at Caernarvon Castle they 'had a little collation in the ruins consisting of biscuits and raisins which Charles got at the grocers and what we could not eat, he flung down from the Castle for the benefit of the little dirty Caernarvon brats.' 'A dull, and *unclean* town'. The summit of Snowdon was 'extremely cold and reminded one chiefly of a London fog on Christmas Eve'. This analogy is no longer appropriate, at least as far as London is concerned! The New Sights, the railway bridges, left her 'surprised, astonished and edified at Mr. Telford's wonderful performances'.

The same hotels still provide for much of the same sort of tourist. (Booking ahead was advisable). 'Six young Germans who found something to laugh at in everything that occurred' and one of whom had to 'endure all manner of little practical jokes'; 'four dear fat elderly tourists with 'uglies' on their heads and opera glasses in their hands were quite determined to see all they could'. There was a regular circuit —the Bulkeley Arms, Beaumaris; the Victoria Hotel, Llanberis; the Goat at Beddgelert. The comments varied from 'very good cook and very civil servants' to 'little attendance of any sort . . . a little unpleasant looking sort of bread pudding sent up each day' to 'I have quite made up my mind to spend my honeymoon at Beddgelert'.

The 'locals' included the *gentry*; Sir Richard Williams Bulkeley reputed to be a second edition of 'the Marquis de Carabas in these parts' (Thackeray's *The Book of Snobs,* 1846); the *clergy* 'the English service . . . at one o'clock'. There were three clergymen, when they did appear; I decided Welshies and one something betwixt the two'.

Today's hurried postcard and instant photo are usually less amusing and certainly less revealing than this exceptionally entertaining and perceptive diary and sketches. I wish there were still ferries across the Straits and I am sorry she thought £500 a piece ill-spent on the '2 enormous stone lions' on the approach to the railway bridge that crosses it. Augusta clearly loved North Wales as I do and I only hope she *did* eventually return for the promised honeymoon at Beddgelert: 'Il mio sposo shall fish, and I shall draw by his side in the most approved and loverlike manner, but *it must be fine weather'.* (My italics). He would have been a very fortunate man.

Shirley Anglesey

London, August 12th 1853

BEING the quintessence of punctuality, (that is to say having been brought up by my Aunt Kate) as the clock struck half eight I was booted and spurred and ready to hop into the cab which was to convey Charles, Cara and myself with a carpet bag apiece to the Euston Square station en route to Chester. It was my first introduction to this gigantic structure and its bustling, fussing, rushing, jostling, pushing, chattering, confusing, and confounding assemblage of people with 'wide awakes' and caps of every hue and shape, and plaids and shawls enough to keep a Siberian winter out. Everybody really looked as if they were bidding adieu to London and its fogs, for a longer space of time than usual, and that with no bad will. For our travelling companions we had two Irish snobs with shirt frills as big as themselves, caps of the ugliest description and waistcoats of the shortest!

A white tied individual of the 'half starved curate' genus made up our party. He had evidently bid adieu to his sermons and his flock and made up his mind to enjoy himself whilst he could. With the exception of having one leg shorter than the other, he was like most other men and he has my best wishes for his welfare here and hereafter. At Chester we left the train and the shirt frills and turned into a magnificent dining room where we regaled the inner man with a substantial dinner, and had the pleasure of witnessing Lord Gough occupied in a

similar manner. Our hunger satisfied, we stepped into an open fly, and desired the coachman to drive us round the Town in which I must confess I was very considerably disappointed. The 'rows' are curious certainly but it all looks dull, dilapidated and dreary and I found myself breathing an inward prayer, that I might never find myself compelled to live at Chester. We went over the Cathedral where the service was being performed and stood for a ¼ of an hour in the cloisters meditating on departed monks etc. and listening to the swelling sounds of the well played organ which Cara observed was 'purifying her soul'. It was certainly very fine and we turned away reluctantly. The Castle, the Suspension Bridge, the Race course and the river Dee were all visited in turn, and then returning to the station we proceeded by the 5 o'clock train to Birkenhead. A large hotel adjoins the station and we there found a sitting room looking out upon the Mersey and reminding one strongly of a dining room at Blackwell. A thick mist concealed Liverpool which is just across the river. Charles sallied forth to see the Docks. Cara took a nap and I did my best to follow her example.

August 13th

UP, DRESSED, breakfasted, bonnetted and down on the pier at ½ 10, where we were told we should find the porter who had preceded us with our luggage, but 'sorry' a porter could we see, or anything approaching to a box or carpet bag and, leaving us there, Charles sped back to the Hotel, in search of the missing articles. Minutes passed away, and so did a quarter of an hour, and so did half an hour, and no Charles, and no porter made their appearance! We began to think about missing the steamer altogether, and were discussing the probabilities thereof, when a man came up and touching his forelock informed us we were to return to the Hotel, that our luggage had been taken by mistake to the 'Amerikay' ship which was lying in

The Euston Square Station   [*H.M.S.O.*]

the river, and was to sail at one o'clock, that 'the gentleman has gone after it', that we were too late for the steamer, that no other steamer went that day, and having delivered himself of that pleasing intelligence he turned upon his heel leaving us in a state of dismay. We walked up and down in the Hotel Garden for some considerable time waiting for Charles' return and at last he came and reported the success of his mission, though it was with much difficulty that he had been able to recapture our property, which the porter had taken with other luggage. Charles was not allowed to go on board and was required to describe most accurately the different packages, their direction etc. He never stopped to think that mine could have been directed with my own name but vowed they all had 'Thomas' on them, and accordingly everything was produced but my unlucky bag, for which they searched far and wide and then said it could not be there, and that the only carpet bag which *had* been there had been sent off in some tender as it belonged to Lady Greenock of 4 Chester Square. It suddenly flashed across Charles' mind that I might have used one of Lady G's cards for my direction, which was just the case and what was more, I had most stupidly forgotten to scratch out her name. The card had turned, I suppose, and my modest little 'A.P. Birkenhead' had been completely overlooked! A lesson to all travelling spinsters to direcct their boxes fully and carefully. It was much more than I deserved to see my brown bag reappear emulating he far famed 'black box'. The Hotel keeper was so penitent and so extremely civil, offering to pay the difference of the railway fare, to give us a dinner gratis and I know not what besides and they ended by sending a man over to Liverpool to ascertain whether there would be any other steamer later in the day or whether we should be obliged to rail back to Chester. He brought us back a favourable answer in half an hour and reported that 'the Menai' would leave Liverpool at ½ after 4. Dinner was ordered at 2, and *pour passer le temps* we got a fly and drove to the docks or rather the would-be docks, upon which upwards of a million has already been spent, and they are not half completed, for want of further funds. In prospect of these docks a large town has been laid out, squares and streets without end, churches and shops all closed, and a large park with a very handsome piece of water. It has the appearance of a city of the dead and made one quite melancholy to look upon.

From thence we went to the Emigrant's House and went all over the 'New Zealander' an emigrant ship which was to sail in a few days. Nothing could exceed the order and cleanliness which reigned everywhere, and all the arrangements for their comfort were most admirable. They have a very nice little church in the precincts, or rather I should say, a Hall fitted up as a church. The ship was to contain 400 emigrants, and certainly they had not much room to spare, their little berths were like so many little narrow coffins closely wedged together and I could not but fancy the poor wretches in a storm. There were all manner of ingenious devices for making a great deal of room out of a very little, the tables being made to push up and down from the ceiling etc.

There were two huge chests from 'Apothecaries Hall' in the cabin, called the Hospital. A doctor was examining them all when we were there, to ascertain whether they had all been vaccinated. We spoke to a very attractive looking girl who told us she came from Oban. She said she had a husband, but no children, and she did not seem to have quite made up her mind whether she was going to Australia *con amore* or not. She had such pretty eyes and such a sweet smile and countenance that we quite lost our hearts to her. At 4 p.m. we went on board the Menai Steamer which was to take us to Beaumaris; we had prepared our minds for a cold and rough passage, but it proved quite the contrary,

'The Departure'

and we had nothing to complain of, but the thick mist which concealed the coast most effectually. Our chief amusement on board was watching and listening to six young Germans who were evidently on pleasure bent, and a more happy joyous assemblage I never saw. They found something to laugh at in every thing that occurred and there was one whom they called the 'Landsmann',* who had to endure all manner of little practical jokes and seemed the scapegoat of the whole party, but he bore it all with most perfect good humour and showed off an immense mouth to the greatest advantage. They were each provided with a water proof coat, a walking stick and a diminutive carpet bag, from which they perpetually extracted cigars.

They were very undecided as to whether they should land at Beaumaris or proceed to Bangor, and I was quite depressed, when they settled on the latter course, and regretted beyond measure, that we had been *too shy* to enter into converse with them. At 9 o'clock we touched the pier at Beaumaris and took up our quarters at the 'Bulkeley Arms' just facing the sea with a very pretty view of the Carnarvonshire mountains.

Sunday, August 14th

WE WENT to church at 11 and heard a very good sermon from a Mr. Jones, after which we perambulated this cheerful, pretty looking place. In the evening Charles and I walked to the Garth Ferry, about 2 miles off from whence we got a view of the Menai Bridge, but too distant a view for poor blind me fully to appreci-

---

*fellow countryman, compatriot.

ate the wonders thereof. On our return we joined Cara on the pier and imbibed a good mouthful of fresh sea air, and diverted ourselves in observing a Scotch family with a boy in a kilt and beautiful long hair blowing about his shoulders.

Monday, August 15th

GOT up very early by *mistake* and was out on the pier at half after six. After breakfast Cara and I attempted some sketching but we were boiled and stewed in a hot sun and I only made a vile daub. In the afternoon we drove to Penmôn Priory, such a pretty secluded spot with the remains of a church, a dormitory and a refectory. Those monks were very knowing old Gentlemen, and evidently knew what was good in every way! From thence we went to the Lighthouse, close to Puffin Island, off which the 'Rothesay Castle' steamer from Liverpool was lost. We had some talk with the Lighthouse man who seemed to have a very snug berth there, a most comfortable looking house with a nice Garden, but he was evidently one of the dissatisfied ones of this world and complained much of the extreme loneliness, though there were two men employed there and plenty to do. I recommended him strongly to get a wife, to make it cheerful, but he only shook his head at my advice. In the evening we walked round the Old Castle and saw Sir Richard Williams Bulkeley's place, Baron Hill. He is a second edition of the Marquis de Carabas in these parts and is moreover member for the county. He must have an uncommonly pretty view from his windows tho' it must be bleak enough in winter. We saw his pretty yacht go by in the morning, to the Isle of Man. The 'Bulkeley Arms' Hotel, at which we are, is a most thoroughly

The City of Bangor

comfortable one, and they can moreover boast of a very good cook and very civil servants. Our room with a bow window overlooks the sea and the pier, which is paid by subscription, twopence for everybody! There are a number of little pleasure boats which enliven the scene and a vast assemblage of idle men and boys who add considerably to the picturesque, lounging over the wall. I must not forget to mention that on opening my shutters this morning, the first persons I beheld were our 6 beloved Germans all standing near the pier watching for the steamer which was to *re*convey them to Liverpool. They must have come from Bangor last night.

Tuesday, August 16th

THE morning opened cheerily upon us with a bright sun, and we intended to get a sailing boat and go down to see the Menai and Britannia Bridges returning afterwards to Bangor, but when we had written our letters and were ready to start, a change came o'er the spirit of the dream, the clouds gathered heavily overhead, the calm waters grew troubled and then down came the rain. Charles decided the sailing expedition to be out of the question and we consequently got an open carriage with a hood, in which Cara and I were comfortably ensconced, and Charles mounted the box. It was a very pretty drive skirting the sea all the way, and passing many pretty houses built on the bank which rises rather steeply from the sea. One little neat domain which attracted our attention was built, the coachman said, by 'an old maid' and she lives there now. I do not envy her the winter, but at present she looks uncommonly snug and pretty. The largest of these species of villas belongs to Sir John Williams. It is just completed, and intended, quoth the coachy for Lady Williams and her two daughters, for the property which is considerable, will go to his nephew and he has built this new place as a jointure house. The gardens which were one blaze of flowers were very prettily laid out in the Italian style and there were terraces down to the water's edge. Adjoining this is a small place belonging to Colonel Williams, the member for Marlow, but no relation of his neighbour's Sir John. Another mile brought us to the Menai Bridge which we drove over and a most stupendous affair it is. I was hardly cognizant of its immense size till we saw a carriage on the bridge, which looked more like a spider on a large beam than anything else. The iron work looks very light and graceful but the piers are rather heavy and ugly. We soon reached Bangor which is built in a hollow between two mountains and has a picturesque effect with Penrhyn Castle as a background. The owner thereof, Colonel Douglas Pennant is Lord Paramount here, and owns the 'Penrhyn Arms' Hotel which is on a very large scale and apparently most comfortable. There is an extremely pretty garden, brilliant with scarlet geraniums and overlooking the sea and the place from which all the slate is shipped, the quarry is some way up the country and the slate is brought to the sea by a tram road. It is quite ridiculous to see the slate, slate, slate, whichever way you turn your head and the palings even, strips of slate instead of wood. Colonel Pennant gets seventy thousand by it. After dinner, which bye the bye was a very good one and consisted of giblet soup, salmon, mutton cutlets, and three sweets, to say nothing of vegetables, cheese etc., we sallied forth to see something of Bangor, but we did not get far which was owing partly to Cara's feeling rather heavy which was attributed to an additional cutlet which she partook of, and partly to a heavy

Penrhyn Castle from Garth Point on the Menai Straits

shower of rain, which however Cara declared would be nothing and pulling up the hood of her cloak she deliberately squatted herself under a tree, and assured us the rain could not reach her!! But we unfortunately were not equally impervious, and after some time we succeeded in persuading her we should be rather more comfortable with a roof over us!!

Later in the evening notwithstanding the rain Cara and I walked into the town to forage for some books and found 'Gilbert Gurney' and James' Old Oak Chest to while away the wet evening. An amiable Harper played most exquisitely in the Hall for an hour or so. The waiter tells us he comes here every evening and is the best Harper in the country, certainly his playing was wonderfully good and so was his instrument. He comes round to the different rooms after his performance and we agreed we had enjoyed a very good concert for a shilling. I dare say he gets a good little sum, for this Hotel is perfectly full as well as 2 houses opposite belonging to it; but the Landlord tells us that for 8 months out of the year they have nothing whatever to do. They have been obliged to turn away several parties today, and we have reason to congratulate ourselves that Charles wrote for rooms, from Beaumaris.

Wedy. August 17th.

AFTER breakfast Cara and I made a sketch from the Hotel Garden and at one o'clock we made our way down to the station and started per train for Conway which we reached in the course of an hour and a half, and entering the refreshment room adjoining the station, we made a cold chicken look very foolish and then we bent our steps to the suspension and Tubular Bridges built on to the old castle in a very ingenious way. They are alongside of each other and add greatly to the effect of the *tout ensemble.* After being duly surprised, astonished and edified at Mr. Telford's wonderful performances, we explored the Castle which was built by Edward 1st in 1284, and a very fine old ruin it is and so prettily situated with the sea running at the foot of it. There is a very pretty view from the battlements which I endeavoured to commit to paper. How surprised old King Edward would have been could he have foreseen that a railway train would rush through a large iron box, under the walls of his castle!

The towers at each end of the bridges are made to harmonise with the old castle and at a little distance, the new suspension bridge has the appearance of a drawbridge up to the Castle gate. It was a glorious day and we remained some time on the turrets gazing at the pretty view before us and inhaling the fresh sea breezes, but 'pleasure vanisheth, alas!' and we resorted again to our convenient railroad and returned to the Head Quarters at Bangor. We were haunted when we set out, whilst there, and when we returned from Conway by four dear, fat, elderly tourists, who with 'uglies' on their heads and opera glasses in their hands, were quite determined to see all they could, and no doubt, a great deal more besides. We caught the last glimpse of these very

Picnic in the Rain

Rev. John Parker, Watercolour

[*N.L.W.*]

interesting people as they stept into a one horse 'shay', and I felt most deeply for the unfortunate horse which was to drag these 4 precious souls, well covered with fat and smothered in wittles.

Thursday, August 18th

U p early, walked to the post in a very hopeful state of mind, returned, dejected and spiritless, even a tour in North Wales is improved by the occasional receipt of a letter; *ésperons toujours.* At 1.15 we set off per train to Carnarvon, did not take an umbrella, and so of course down came the rain but we got into some old windows of the Castle and sketched for more than an hour. I fancy we must have had rather a comical effect in our niches aloft, for I observed the different people point us out as part of the show to their less observant companions.

This is another of Edward 1st's castles, making the third we have seen in the last few days. Those Welsh mountaineers were well protected at all events. We had a little collation in the ruins, consisting of biscuits and raisins which Charles got at a grocer's, and what we could not eat, he flung down from the Castle for the benefit of the little dirty Carnarvon brats. Before leaving this dull and *unclean* town we strolled down to the pier, where I was very much amused watching the proceedings of the people waiting to cross in the ferry boat. There was one nice little Welshwoman, the very pink of neatness, she was attired in the blue plaid of the country with a cap as white as snow and her hat which crowned it, was most cannily enveloped in a blue pocket handkerchief—to keep the sea water from it, I suppose. She sat there on the boat with the composure of a little Duchess but no drawing of mine could do the little dear justice. The rest of the assemblage were of quite a different order, men, who had evidently been taking a holiday and taking a little something besides, which just elevated their spirits, sufficiently to make them amusing, and their stupid faces and gesticulations as they harangued the company were irresistibly ridiculous. I was quite sorry when the bell was sounded, the cables loosed and the boat steamed away. We got to our hotel at ½ 8 and were not sorry to find ourselves at dinner.

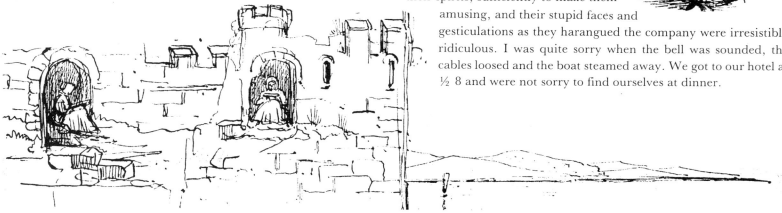

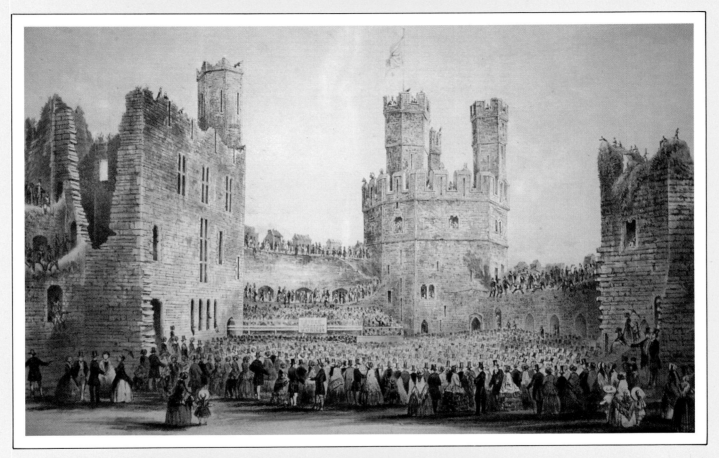

The Interior of Carnarvon Castle
(Jubilee of the British & Foreign Bible Society August 3 1853)

[Gwynedd Archives]

Friday, August 19th

AT 11 o'clock, this morning, we walked down to the quay and found a little pleasure boat awaiting us, which Charles had engaged to take us to the Menai Bridge. The sea was very smooth and we found the air delicious. We were fully impressed with the enormous height of the bridge and the immense span thereof. When under it, I don't know that I ever felt so insignificant before. The tide prevented our going to the Tubular bridge in the boat, so we landed and walked on, till we reached the wondrous thing. A train came rolling through as we stood beneath it and the sounds were something terrific. We were invited to walk through the tube and a guide was at hand to conduct us, but neither Cara nor I relished the idea. At each end, there are two enormous stone Lions, which cost 500£ apiece, it seemed to me the 2000£ might have been spent to more advantage, but no doubt I am wrong. We saw the Clarence Paget's house, facing the river and just above the bridge. It did not look particularly pretty, but I dare say, they have a nice view of the opposite coast from their windows. We found on nearing Bangor that the water would not serve us for landing on the pier and we were forced to scramble up the side of a brig and thus make our way up to the quay. The wind was blowing and the ladder a steep and long one. *More*, I need not add, as I have no doubt the fertile imaginations of my 3 dear sisters will fill up what is wanting!

Back at the Penrhyn Arms, we fortified ourselves with some luncheon and packing up our traps bid adieu to these very comfortable quarters. Another large party departed a minute before us. 9 children of all ages and sizes, a governess, a papa and Mama and another lady to say nothing of the domestics. It was very amusing to see them stowed away in the cars, one of which had a pair of horses and held eight very comfortably. I had the curiosity to peep into the visitors book to see what names this *small* family rejoiced in, and I found

'Countess of Dunmore and family' and The Honble H and Lady Emily Vesey and party, so that they proved to be combined forces. We now had occasion to congratulate ourselves on the smallness of our luggage, as our bags just fitted into the car and off we trotted at a tremendous pace up hill and down again, jostle and jolt and jolt and jostle. The only incident however was the falling out of my fated brown bag, but as usual I recovered it, none the worse for its tumble. Llanberis and its surrounding mountains soon broke upon our delighted eyes. Snowdon had got a mist over its summit; it occasionally lifted its veil, but would not show its face completely. We found our destination, the Victoria Hotel, a slate coloured house with a red flag flying. A few dirty straggling cottages compose the village of Llanberis. Having deposited our traps, we sallied forth and meeting a little boy who offered to guide us to the Waterfall, we followed him, and found ourselves opposite a torrent of rather a picturesque nature. In going

The Britannia Bridge   [*H.M.S.O.*]

over the top of it and stepping from rock to rock, my foot slipped in some unaccountable way and I found myself immersed in the stream. Charles who was following me rushed to the rescue and being once more on my legs I clawed hold of his proffered hand, made one step, and then, in, I slipt again but this time it was not quite such a complete bath, tho' I could hardly get up again for laughing, the boy who was before me stood there with his mouth wide open and the most contrite expression on his face, as tho' he felt he had led me into this mischief and there was Cara on the bank, laughing, as if she never would stop, it was altogether a most absurd scene. I was perfectly saturated, from my bonnet downwards and even the strings of that were perfectly wet, and a pretty figure I cut, walking home again in this dripping state!

I was soon *re*-equipped in dry clothes, and none the worse for my cold bath, beyond a bruise on my elbow and knee. My garments were much the greatest sufferers, and I do not think either of you, my dear sisters would give me a 'thank you' for my green silk gown today. I sent it down to the kitchen fire with all the rest of my things but it was brought up again this morning only half dry. So much for that adventure, which can scarcely be denominated either sentimental or picturesque, we will put it down amongst the acquatics. I did not venture out again after my ducking, but wrapping a plaid round me, to keep off 'a chill', I seated myself at the window and watched the departure of a party of seven men, some on ponies and some on foot, all bound for Snowdon, where they mean to sleep tonight in order to see the sunrise tomorrow morning. I do not envy them their moonlight ride up the Hills, and greatly prefer the thoughts of my warm bed.

Saturday, August 20th

Was not called this morning and consequently slept till an unconsciously late hour, tho' you, in your *civilized* parts would, I dare say, assert ½ after 9 to be about the right time

Llyn Gwynant, near Beddgelert   [*Gwynedd Archives*]

to appear. We mountaineers keep earlier hours, *when* we don't over-sleep ourselves! After breakfast we started with our sketchbooks and Cara on a pony, to explore the 'Pass of Llanberis' and most beautiful it was. I never saw anything so handsomely savage as the scenery here. Huge pieces of rock have been washed from the hills and lie about on each side of the road, a stream gurgles through it and adds greatly to the beauty. *Chemin faisant,* we encountered such a bewitching little Welsh maiden in a grey wide awake, blue jacket and pink skirt with long flowing locks blowing about her shoulders, and such a pretty pair of eyes! It was impossible to resist drawing her and she seemed nothing loth. I had not done much before I was surrounded by little boys, who looked on in the greatest wonderment. They could none of them speak or understand English and the little girl, Margaret Evans, interpreted all they said, which was chiefly expressing their curiosity as to what she 'was to have' for letting me take her picture. They watched my brush every time I dipped it into the paint, as if it was the greatest curiosity in nature. I quite lost my heart to Margaret, and her pretty little ways. She tripped over the brook with her little shoeless feet and took the picture for her mother to see and when she brought it back said with the prettiest of smiles and dimpled cheeks, 'mother says it is much better than I am'. She looked as pleased as Punch, when I gave her a shilling and we parted the greatest of friends. We dined at 4 o'clock and afterwards went to sketch in another direction. Oh 'how lovely the lights and shades are'.

Sunday, August 21st

WE were told that the English service would be performed in a ci-devant* cowhouse, whitewashed and fitted up with seats, at one o'clock, and at that hour, accordingly we went

*former

to church and there we sat, with about 50 people to keep us in countenance till very nearly two o'clock. There were three clergymen, when they did appear, I decided Welshies, and one something betwixt the two. In the evening we clambered over the Hills, and went to bed well tired out.

Monday, August 22nd

UP very early, as the Guides and Ponies were ordered to take us up Snowdon at ½ past 8. It was a most lovely bright morning and Charles and I, with a guide wended our way upwards for about 3 miles enjoying the bright prospect around us. My pony was undoubtedly the most surefooted of its race, and picked its way most deliberately and knowingly over all the loose stones which fill the pathway; about 2 miles from the summit the scene underwent a complete change. We came upon some prodigiously black frowning rocks crowned at the top by a thick mist, flying about in all directions, and we felt most completely and thoroughly in the clouds.

Llanberis Pass

Rev. John Parker, Watercolour

It became extremely cold and reminded one chiefly of a London fog on Christmas Eve. Charles got down to warm himself by walking, enveloped in a plaid, and thus and then we arrived at the top, which is crowned by a large pile of flints in such wise.

We could not see anything but the stones we stood on, and most gladly turned in to a little hut, sort of place, and crouched over a stove, which gradually infused a little warmth into our frozen selves. It seemed perfectly hopeless to wait for a chance of its clearing and having perused a book intended for visitors' names, but full of would be witticisms, acrostics, conundrums etc, 'Why is Snowdon like an Eastern lady?' 'Because she is always veiled', and such like, and wherein, (should any of my beloved friends ere peep) they will find

Well! Oh well!
What lies those guide books tell!

Augusta Pearson.

Not that I ever wrote it. Beware!!
And then, down we came again. It was not very pleasant, as I felt strongly inclined to slip over my pony's head occasionally but as to the much-talked of, and much-written-about, danger, there was none that I could discover.

The guide helped himself up by taking a vigorous hold of my pony's tail, which was much appreciated by poor 'Ginger'. He pointed out a particular hill to us known by the name of 'Congregation Hill'. A young clergyman, Mr. Starr of Northampton, having been lost there 7 years ago—. He left Carnarvon with the view of reaching Snowdon on the Beddgelert side to see the sun rise. He was dissuaded from going without a guide, as the weather was bad, but he declared he knew the road perfectly, and started by himself. Nothing was heard of him for some weeks and the guides at Beddgelert, not finding subsequently that he had been seen on the summit, supposed he had given up the undertaking. About a month afterwards, his mother and 2 sisters arrived in the neighbourhood in search of him; enquiries were made, hundreds of workmen from the quarries were engaged in searching for him, and a reward of £50 offered, but it was not till 5 months afterwards that his bones were found with a handkerchief, purse and watch. There is little doubt, that he mistook his way in the twilight, and fell headlong over the dark precipice where his remains were discovered.

We got back to the Victoria Hotel at 2 and found Cara returned from her sketching expedition. After dinner I went to the hill on which the ruins of Dolbadarn Castle stand, and sketched some little ragged Welsh children, beginning with one, but I was very soon beset with a dozen or more, all clamourous to have their pictures taken. They were one and all most picturesque in their dirt and their rags and they sang to me in Welsh and an English 'tea total' song, which they said they had learnt at Chapel. I presented my 'model' with sixpence with which she scampered off in great glee, but soon returned announcing that her mother would give me back the 6d if I would let her have the picture, and I was at some trouble to make the little imp understand that I wanted to take the little Welsh girl back to England.

Tuesday.

LLANBERIS is so attractive that we prolong our stay from day to day, and feel most forcibly the charms of being tied to no-one and nowhere!! I went out sketching after breakfast and again in the afternoon, which affords no materials for journalising, as only one thing happened, and that, woe betide me is the loss of my eyes! They must have dropped somewhere near the waterfall, but I made a fruitless search. Thank my stars, Cara came with two pairs, so that I am somewhat comforted, by the loan of them. Charles made a second peregrination to Snowdon, and this time had a very clear view from the summit. This hotel is full to repletion, and we get but little attendance of any sort. A stupid looking Irish waiter, and one waitress, with a couple of slovenly looking drabs under her, are all in the way of servants, and the rushing and running and ringing of bells, is something astonishing. Dinner occupies about a couple of hours, having to wait so long between the courses that I find time to do some drawing *en attendant* and withal the poor hard-worked maid is so civil that Charles can only find in his heart to remonstrate by ringing the bell for five minutes together. The cooking is *comme ça*. We have had a little unpleasant looking sort of bread pudding sent up each day. I maintain it is the same identical one, and that we shall have it, till we make up our minds to eat it, which luckily, hunger, does not drive us to, as there is always a little tart, which is not so bad, and some jelly glasses with a little lump of jelly stuck at the top of each, just fitting into the wide front of each glass.

Vivat the cooking!
Floreat Llanberis!

Wednesday, August 24th

THE car, which was to jolt us away from this majestic wilderness was ordered at 11, but in these parts, everything and everybody are invariably two hours after their time, and we were quite weary of waiting for our Shandrydan, before it made its appearance. At last a very crazy looking vehicle drove up to the door, something between a phaeton and a pony chaise, into which we packed ourselves and property and were soon in a very different scene, exchanging the rugged, frowning 'awe' striking rocky mountains for hills and vales, running streams, and green pastures. I was perfectly enchanted with the drive from Llanberis to Beddgelert, and was quite sorry when we came to a stop, on arriving at the Goat Hotel, which was cram full but Charles' precaution of writing the day before had secured our getting rooms, and most comfortable ones they are. An immense improvement upon Llanberis! And our dinner seemed perfectly delicious, from the contrast. Directly we had swallowed it, and without waiting to digest it we rushed down the Vale of Glynant, and came upon the most exquisitive views I ever beheld. It made me wild, to think I could not carry away 50 sketches, which would do justice to those lovely blue distances, and as 'fools rush in, where angels fear to tread', I was down on my camp stool and daubing away in no time and for the first five minutes I was in ecstacy, but then, oh then, if swearing could have availed, I really think I must have indulged in a few hard words at the midges which stung my face, and my throat, and my hands, till I was almost out of my mind, and it was quite out of the question to sit there any longer, though I really did remain till my face was crimson!

Cara was also drawing, at a little distance, and I could hear her groaning and bewailing, as well as myself, and at last we decamped from the scene of action.

The pursuit of art under difficulties.

Thursday morning.

I WAS up with the dawn, for we had seen so many lovely views that I meant to try half a dozen at least in the course of the day, but alas down came the rain and sent all my intentions to the 'Right about face' but as this is the first wet day, we have had, we have no right to grumble. In the afternoon the clouds dispersed, the sun shone brightly forth and we lost no time in hurrying on our bonnets. Charles got a pony for Cara and told us to prepare our minds for going 5 miles out and 5 back again. With the pony to rest us, we were nothing loth and marched stoutly on, but, the clearing was nothing but a mockery, a snare, and a delugion, for deluged we were all in a minute. Cara and I sheltered ourselves as well as we could with a wall and an umbrella, whilst Charles, protected the unhappy saddle.

After a while a car came rattling by in which sat two jolly farmers, and they were moved with compassion at the sight of two such wet-begone damsels and benevolently offered us a lift, which we most thankfully accepted, and we jogged back to the Goat, most gratefully —Charles following on the pony.

Friday.

DEVOTED to spoiling a great deal of paper, in the vain attempt to depict these lovely mountains. Lost my temper occasionally as was assailed by another batch of midges. In the afternoon I went in quest of Gelert's grave and found an old stone overhung by bushes and surrounded by a paling in the midst of a large field and in sight of Snowdon's Peak. Me-wonders whether the far-famed dog really ever did exist here but I am rather sceptical on the subject, particularly after reading that this tale seems originally to have come

from the East, where almost all beautiful stories have their birth. It is said to be engraven on a rock at Limerick; it is told in an old English romance; it is repeated in France; and it is the subject of a Persian Drama!! And there is a Welsh adage, which alludes to this legend, 'He repents as much, as the man who killed the dog'.

At Pont Aber Glaslyn, where we sketched yesterday, they have an old story about the bridge there, sometimes called the Devil's bridge, because the black gentleman, once proposed to the neighbouring in-habitants to build them a bridge on the condition that he should take possession of the first who crossed it, for his trouble. The bargain was made and the bridge soon appeared, and the people, in fulfilment of the contract, dragged a dog to the spot, and whipped him over to his Satanic Majesty's care.

My ♡ leapt with joy, this morning at the sight of our 4 never to be forgotten dear old travelling spinsters. I am quite glad they should have got thus far in a good state of preservation. I am not quite sure that one did not look a shade redder in the face than when I saw her last, but I dare say the poor dear has not kept her shade on as much as she should have done. Talking of redness, (or rather, writing of it) the barmaid here has got the most brilliantly red nose eyes ever rested upon, but she evidently considers herself the belle of Beddgelert and her toilette is *ravissante*, a most 'twitching' brown sassnet bow making up for a deficiency of hair.

Saturday.

WE left the Goat Hotel at Beddgelert with great regret. The landlady and all her satellites were the most civil people I ever encountered, and there was one waitress in particular whom I much grieved to part with. She rejoiced, I believe, in the name of Ellen Thomas, and from the remarks made upon her in the visitors' book, I should imagine she had won more hearts than mine. The most good-natured, laughing Welshwoman you can fancy, and so fat, oh, so fat. She was quite a character, evidently, and certainly a very amusing one. She enquired very tenderly when we were 'coming again' and bye the bye I have quite made up my mind to spend my Honeymoon at Beddgelert. *Il mio sposo* shall fish, and I shall draw by his side, in the most approved and lover-like manner, but it must be fine weather.

We had rather a rainy drive of ten miles ere we reached the 'Oakley Arms' at Tan-y-Bwlch, situated on an eminence and overlooking the Vale of Ffestiniog with a very pretty river running through it. It was decided that we should take up our quarters here for Sunday instead of proceeding to Ffestiniog, and we partook of some excellent hare soup (which had a novel feature in it, i.e. large onions, stuck full of cloves), and some mutton chops, succeeded by an apple tart and cream, after which we made an expedition to Plas Tan-y-Bwlch, a place belonging to Mrs. Oakley. The house, which looks a very old one, is situated very like the Gnoll with woods behind and around it and on an eminence likewise with a very broad terrace in front of the house, from which we

had a very pretty view over the valley. The place was in the most perfect order and we gathered that the fortunate possessor of all we saw, and a very great deal more, this hotel included, is a widow, aged 50 and with no children. Her husband has been gathered to his fathers for the last 20 years and from what I can make out she seems to live quite alone. I wonder how she has managed to resist all the entreaties she must have had to try the matrimonial line, a second time. Having admired all this fair widow's possessions, we proceeded in a car, three miles on the Harlech road to a waterfall called Rhaiadr Du, or the black cataract. The depth of the fall is about 40 feet, and a very beautiful one it is. The dingle in which it is situated is not the least pretty part, though we saw it under a somewhat unfavourable aspect as the rain came down rather smartly, and we were fain obliged to peep at the beauties, from under umbrellas. At a quarter of a mile's distance the Ravenfall is to be seen, equally beautiful and grand. On dit, that Lord Lyttleton, when sojourning in these parts, wrote to his friend, 'that with the woman one loves, with the friend of one's heart, and a study of books, one might pass an age in this vale, and think it a day'. It seemeth to me that his Lordship was rather exigeant; what could he have desired more than love, friendship, and occupation, to make even a desert habitable, and much less this pretty cheerful valley.

Sunday.

WHETHER it was owing to being out so much in the air, or what, I know not, but this morning I slept till some shamefully late hour, and should have snoozed much longer had not Cara kindly broken in upon my slumbers, with the terrible announcement of its being ten o'clock, and the sun streaming into the room to increase my feelings of shame and remorse. Fortunately the Service did not commence till half after eleven. The church at Maentwrog, a village ½ a mile off, is the tidiest church I have seen in Wales, the singing, most wonderfully good and the clergyman totally *un*Welsh. There seemed a great many English visitors, indeed, I think the congregation was entirely English and the sermon was on behalf of the Church pastoral aid society, but alas for the collection, my purse was not in my pocket, or there is no saying what I might not have deposited in the plate!!! After dinner, we took a long walk up the Vale of Ffestiniog, and were enchanted all the way we went, first with the stream (in which there is first rate fishing) then with the heath covered hills and the wooded banks beneath them and last tho' not least, with the most picturesque old stone bridges, which we fully intend to sketch next time we come this way! I looked through an old book I found on the bookshelf here, entitled the London Gazette for 1813, and found so many names and things familiar to me, such as the announcement of Mrs. Bosanquet's first marriage to Mr. Ganssen; the birth of Captain Douglas! a letter from Sir Richard Bickeston, another from Sir Philip Broke's father announcing to the Admiralty the capture of the Chesapeake, and many interesting letters from the Duke of Wellington, with the returns of the dead and wounded after the battle of Vittoria. For want of something better this was my 'Sunday reading' and very interesting I found it. 'Tea and turn out', closely followed by Turn in, for tomorrow, we have a long day's journey before us, and must be up and stirring at half after five, so *felicissima notte,* dear sisters three, May you slumber sweetly, and dream of me.

Monday.

I ACTUALLY opened my eyes at 4 this morning, but that being a little sooner than I had intended, I coaxed them, into, closing again till, I was called at ½ 5, when the sun was shining gloriously and I was up and dressed and ready to start in no time. We devoured some breakfast with a degree of speed that would have sent Uncle Edmund into hysterics, and then started in a car from Bala. We had so fully made up our minds for rain that both Cara and I were swaddled up in such innumerable shawls, that when it came to walking up the hills, we found ourselves incomodiously large and heavy, and panted and puffed and looked and felt as if we had 18 stone at least to put in motion, but it had the effect of keeping off the rain for several hours and we drove up to the Hotel at Bala at 11 o'clock and learnt that a coach from Dolgelly would be up in a moment. To decide upon taking places in it, to get our letters from the Post office and to buy a bag full of biscuits, was the work of no time and we found ourselves much to our amusement perched on the outside of the said coach, in company with some other tourists, and now came the time when we hugged our wittles to our hearts, and looked with kindly gratitude upon each and all of our infinite wraps, for torrents of rain came down, and the drippings from all the umbrellas added considerably to the wetness of the transaction; so much so, that when we stopped to change horses at Corwen, Charles put us inside. Just as we were nearing this said town, the coach suddenly pulled up with a twist and a jerk and a cry of 'Oh! Stop, Oh! Stop' assailed our ears, in the most piteous of accents and on looking down to see from whom these sounds proceeded, I saw a female figure hanging on to a rearing horse, with the girth broken, and in another instant another girl rode up, and jumping off her horse rushed to her sister's assistance, and joined in the cries of 'Do come somebody' upon which two of the men outside the coach jumped down to the rescue of youth and beauty, for they were both particularly handsome girls, with such bright complexions and black hair, tumbling about in sweet negligé amid the wet and the fright. The cavaliers led the horse on whilst the young maiden followed on foot, the other sister remounted and they were not long in arriving at the hotel where we were partaking of some luncheon. The young ladies, said it was a young horse but they had never known it take fright at the coach before. A third sister and a young man were in advance and quite unconscious of the scene enacted a few yards behind them. We

could not discover the names of these beauteous damsels and could only gather they were strangers, staying in the neighbourhood. Their attire was very fantastic, and consisted of grey wideawakes bound with blue ribbon and long blue ends pendant, a plaid shawl put scarf-wise over their shoulders and a black skirt completed their toilette.

Not being on the whole a correct portrayer of horses, I almost fear my animals do not look *quite the thing!* But as I have said before, I leave what is wanting to your joint imaginations, and in this case you must exercise them chiefly in supplying a seat for one distressed female, who is I know not where.

At three o'clock we drove up to the door of the 'Hand Hotel' at Llangollen, the celebrated valley of that name we had passed through in a semi dormant sort of state, and hardly able to judge through the rain of any of its beauties and as to Llangollen itself! 'Ach a mi!' what a dirty hole, full of squeaking pigs and quarrelling children, to say nothing of an immense number of noisy half inebriated shopkeepers

from Chester, who had come with an excursion train, with a band to make a day's holiday at Llangollen and who, nothing damped by all the wet, were actually dancing in a sort of tea garden place, in front of the Inn.

The rooms at the 'Hand' were all engaged, and we therefore adjourned to the Royal Hotel where we certainly found rooms, tho' not of a very attractive order, and we sallied forth as soon as we could, and clambered up to the ruins of an old Castle and from thence to Valle Crucis Abbey, which has a spectacle quite worth seeing. The ruins are wonderfully preserved and the tombstones. There was a very intelligent cicerone, in the shape of a 'decayed lady' who lives in a neat little cottage close by, and does the Honours of the place to perfection, not excluding the grateful and graceful curtsy when she feels some silver in the palm of her hand. It was dark when we returned to our regal abode and Charles congratulated himself much upon having passed so much of the time, which we were doomed to spend in this dismal Dirtery. The tea and tea cake with some broiled duck, was not so bad either, and we went to bed in a better humour, without having seen Plas Newydd, the far famed abode of the two ladies, who are now being *parodied* by a Miss Solly and a Miss Andrews, but somehow, we could not work ourselves up to any enthusiasm either for the present, or the past, not sufficient even, to pay a man a shilling for showing us a triangular tomb in the Churchyard, where, saith the Guide book Lady Elinor Butler, Miss Ponsonby and their faithful domestic are buried. Peace be to their remains.

Tuesday, August 30th.

MADE another early start in a car to the station at Llangollen road, five miles from the town itself, and bid adieu to 'Sweet Jenny Jones' and all her belongings without the smallest particle of regret. At the station we found a small child and an anxious mother, who had come to ship off this little creature all the way to London by herself. She was going to live with an Aunt, who kept the Magnate Coffee house in the New road, and she had the direction in her hand to show, when she got to town. The poor Mother shed many tears, but the child seemed quite delighted with the novelty of the whole thing. We could not, unfortunately, be of any use to the little creature, as we were to change trains at Wolverhampton, but I hope she reached the Magnate in safety. Our journey today was one series of changing railways and it was truly wonderful that we lost none of our goods in all the moves. We tore thro' Birmingham from one station to another in a cab and for the life of me, could not have dis-

tinguished it from any London thoroughfare. We snapped up some buns and tea at Wolverton and we reached No. 19 Eaton Place South somewhere between 5 and 6 o'clock, without further adventure, and with very much regret on my part that our most agreeable and enjoyable tour had come to an end, *mais, cette est la vie humaine,* and I shall now dear sisters take leave of you for the present, but not without calling to your notice the extreme kindness and goodness of our beloved relations through whose means I have been enabled to spend, as delightful a fortnight and 4 days as ever spinster passed in this world of woe and care! *'Sans souci'* verily and truly, and with everything, that agreeable companionship, lovely scenery, fine weather, good health, and constant occupation (in the daubing way) could do towards making the time pass delightfully by. The sole and only regret was the thought of poor old Fatty and her sprained knee, deprived of all we were enjoying. *'Nul rose sans epine'* saith the writer.

Behold the end of these desultory and wayfaring notes, which will perhaps draw, a shrug of the shoulders from one, a compassionate smile from the other and a comical grin from the third of my loving and beloved Sisterhood. Be that as it may, and Lebewohl.*

Augusta Pearson

---

*—live well.

'My bedroom': 4 Lowndes Square, London SW   [*Augusta Pearson*]

Augusta Pearson, Watercolour

GLOSSARY

Page 10 Carpet Bag: A travelling bag made of carpet.

Euston Square Station: Euston Station was built in 1837. A triumphal Greek Arch and Roman Great Hall was added in 1846-49. The old station was replaced by the present building in 1962-66.

'Wide Awake': A soft felt hat with broad brim and a low crown, so called jokingly because they did not have a 'nap'.

Lord Gough: An eminent military commander in China and India. b. 1779— d. 1869.

A Fly: A light carriage drawn by one horse.

The 'Rows': Several raised and covered galleries running along the sides of four main streets.

The Castle: A Norman Castle strengthened by Edward I which was much altered in the eighteenth century.

The Suspension Bridge: Built in 1852.

The 'Amerikay': An emigrant ship bound for North America. During the mid-nineteenth century 200,000 emigrants sailed each year from the Mersey—the fare cost between £3.50 and £5.

The Menai: Steam packets commenced running from Liverpool to Bangor in 1822.

Page 12 From 1824 William Laird began to invest in Birkenhead which underwent rapid development in the last century. The first docks were opened in August 1847.

This was the first park to be laid out at public expense. The park was designed by Sir John Paxton and laid out in 1843-47.

Medical examination of all emigrants was compulsory after 1849. Vaccination was made compulsory in 1853.

Page 14 The Bulkeley Arms: Built in 1831. Designed by Hansom and Welch.

The Garth Ferry: The ferry between Bangor and Beaumaris was held at this time by Thomas Morgan.

Penmôn Priory: Originally a Celtic Monastic foundation or clasau. It became an Augustinian Priory in the thirteenth century and was dissolved in 1536. The Priory is dedicated to St. Seiriol.

The Rothesay Castle: In 1831 on a journey from Liverpool to Beaumaris this steamer ran into difficulties and struck the Dutchman's Bank, near Penmon. About fifty lost their lives.

Baron Hill: Built by the seventh Lord Bulkeley who died in 1822. Samuel Wyatt was the architect.

Page 16 The Menai Bridge: Designed by Thomas Telford and opened in 1826. The Menai Bridge is considered to be this Scottish engineer's greatest achievement.

The Britannia Bridge: A tubular bridge to carry trains. It was designed by Robert Stephenson and opened on 5 March, 1850. At one time 1500 men were employed in building the bridge. This bridge was destroyed by fire in 1970 and subsequently rebuilt to carry trains and cars.

Penrhyn Castle: G. H. Dawkins Pennant (1763-1840) commissioned Thomas Hopper in 1827 to rebuild the house he had inherited. Penrhyn Castle is considered to be the masterpiece of the Norman Revival in Britain.

The Penrhyn Arms Hotel: Built at the end of the eighteenth century. It became the first home of the University College of North Wales in 1884. The portico can still be seen overlooking the harbour at Hirael, Bangor.

Port Penrhyn constructed in 1801 with a tramway between the quarries in Bethesda and the quay. Steam locomotives were introduced in the 1840s. Slates have been shipped from this site at the mouth of the Cegin near Bangor since 1700.

Page 18 Conway Suspension Bridge: Opened in 1826. Designed by Thomas Telford.

The Tubular Bridge: Opened in 1850 to carry trains. Designed by Robert Stephenson.

'Uglies': A kind of hood or shade attached to the front of a lady's bonnet or hat as a protection to the eyes.

Page 20 'Shay': A carriage of various shapes but usually low and open. A 'shay' is a corruption of 'chaise'.

Wittles: Obsolete form of 'victuals', i.e. food.

Caernarfon Railway: This line was opened to passengers in July 1852.

The ferry boat: The ferry brought people from Anglesey to Caernarfon and vice-versa. A steam ferry was introduced in 1849. In 1853 the fare was 2p each way for adults. Before the ferry set out a horn was blown in Caernarfon to warn passengers of departure.

Blue plaid: Blue woollen cloth was produced in Caernarfonshire.

Page 22   Clarence Paget: Clarence Paget was the son of the Marquess of Anglesey. Plas Newydd was originally a sixteenth century manor house which was greatly altered during the eighteenth century. In he 1790s the west facing entrance was given a more impressive facade and the interior was redesigned in Gothic and classical style by James Wyatt and Joseph Potter of Lichfield.
Brig: A two-masted, square-rigged vessel.

Page 24   Plaid: A long piece of woollen cloth usually with tartan pattern.

Page 26   The old parish church of Llanberis is situated in Nant Peris. Edmund Hyde Hall in his *Description of Caernarvonshire* (1809-1811) describes it as 'a very mean building'. Churches were often whitewashed well into the nineteenth century.
Snowdon could be ascended from Llanberis via Dolbadarn Castle or from the village itself where the path is very steep.

Page 28   'The little hut': Described by Borrow in *Wild Wales* written after his tour in 1854 as 'a rude cabin' where refreshments were sold. He reports that a person lived there throughout the year.
Mr. Starr of Northampton: This was a cause célèbre in the area. The family of the deceased suspected that Mr. Starr had been murdered by one of the guides. An inquest however decided that no foul play had taken place. Despite this Mr. Starr's sister published a book in which she expressed her suspicions concerning the circumstances of her brother's death.
'Tea total': The temperance movement was very strong in non-conformist Wales and was popularised by the singing of teetotal songs in English and Welsh.

Page 30   Shandrydan: A light two wheeled vehicle.
Phaeton: A light four wheeled open carriage.
Pony chaise: A carriage which was usually low, four-wheeled and open drawn by one or two ponies.
The Goat Hotel: George Borrow stayed here the following year and describes it as 'a large and commodious building' but he disliked the clientele!
The Goat was built between 1800 and 1802.

Page 31   Gelert's Grave: A well known legend said to have been created by the Goat Hotel's first landlord, David Prichard. According to the story, Gelert was Llewelyn Fawr's dog. Llewelyn mistakenly believed that Gelert had killed his child and in rage he slaughtered Gelert.
Pont Aber Glaslyn: Until 1895 this was the boundary between Caernarfonshire and Merionethshire. Before the planting of trees at Aberglaslyn during the nineteenth century it was a very rugged barren area.

Page 32   The Oakeley Arms: Built by the Oakeley family of the Tanybwlch Estate. The hotel was the property of the estate.
'A very pretty river . . .': The Dwyryd.
Plas Tan-y-Bwlch: A mansion constructed in the eighteenth century, restored and added to in the nineteenth century.
Mrs. Louisa Jane Oakeley was married to William Griffith Oakeley (d. 1835) the member of the family who first took an interest in the Blaenau slate quarries and in the development of Maentwrog. Mrs. Oakeley was mentally unstable for many years and died in 1879.
Lord Lyttleton visited the area in 1756.
Maentwrog Church: The church patronised by the Tanybwlch family. At this time the rector was David Edwards. The church was rebuilt to a large extent in 1896.

Page 33   The Hotel at Bala: Most probably the White Lion Royal Hotel. There was no rail link between Dolgellau and Bala until 1868.

Page 34   'Ach a mi': A Welsh term of disgust: 'Ach a fi'.
From 1848 visitors could travel by train to Llangollen Road Station.
Valle Crucis Abbey: A Cistercian Abbey, founded in 1201 and dissolved 1536.
Cicerone: Guide.

Page 35   Plas Newydd: Plas Newydd, an eighteenth century black and white house, was for fifty years the home of the famous Ladies of Llangollen. In 1778 two Irish aristocrats Lady Eleanor Butler and Miss Sarah Ponsonby came to live in Llangollen with their maid, Mary Carryl. Their mannish clothes attracted a great deal of attention.